Community Helpers

Astronauts

by Tami Deedrick

Content Consultant:
Dr. John Lawrence
Chief, Operations and Program Support
Johnson Space Center (NASA)

Bridgestone Books

an imprint of Capstone Press

Bridgestone Books are published by Capstone Press
818 North Willow Street, Mankato, Minnesota 56001
http://www.capstone-press.com

Library of Congress Cataloging-in-Publication Data
Deedrick, Tami.
    Astronauts/by Tami Deedrick.
       p. cm.--(Community helpers)
    Includes bibliographical references (p. 24) and index.
    Summary: An introduction to astronauts that examines their tasks, clothing, tools, and
education.
    ISBN 1-56065-727-8
    1. Astronautics--Juvenile literature. 2. Astronauts--Juvenile literature. [1. Astronautics.
    2. Astronauts.] I. Title. II. Series: Community helpers (Mankato, Minn.)
TL793.D374   1998
629.45'0092--dc21

                           97-38177
                             CIP
                               AC

Editorial credits
Editor, Matt Doeden; Cover design and illustrations, Timothy Halldin; Photo research,
Michelle L. Norstad

Photo credits
International Stock, 4
NASA, cover, 6, 8, 10, 12, 14, 18
Visuals Unlimited, 16
Unicorn Stock/Fred Reischl, 20

Table of Contents

Astronauts

An astronaut is a person trained to travel through space. A spacecraft carries astronauts into space. Astronauts study what it is like to live in space. Some astronauts have walked on the moon.

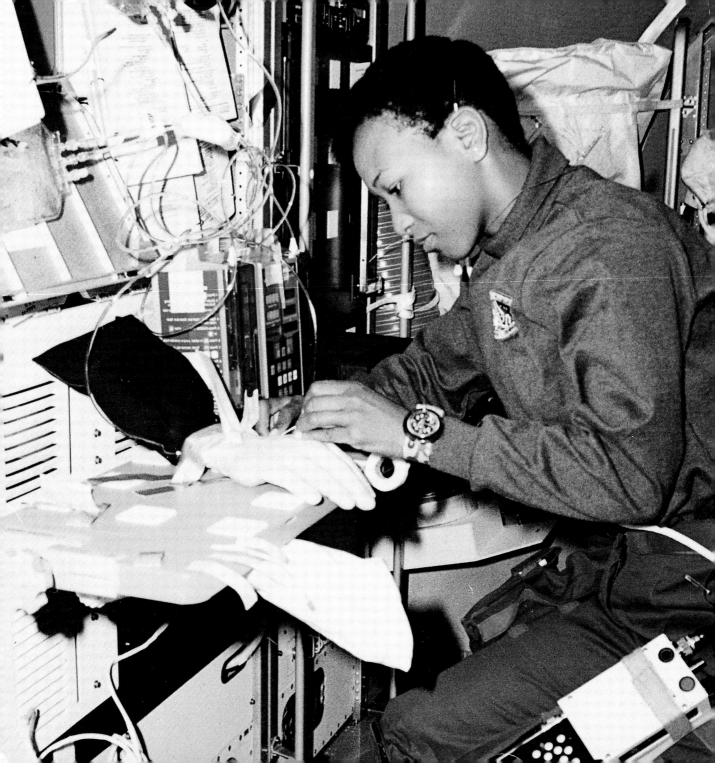

What Astronauts Do

Astronauts spend most of their time learning about space. Sometimes they travel into space. They do experiments in space. An experiment is a test to learn something new.

Different Kinds of Astronauts

Many astronauts are scientists. A scientist is a person who does experiments. Some astronauts are pilots. Pilots fly spacecraft.

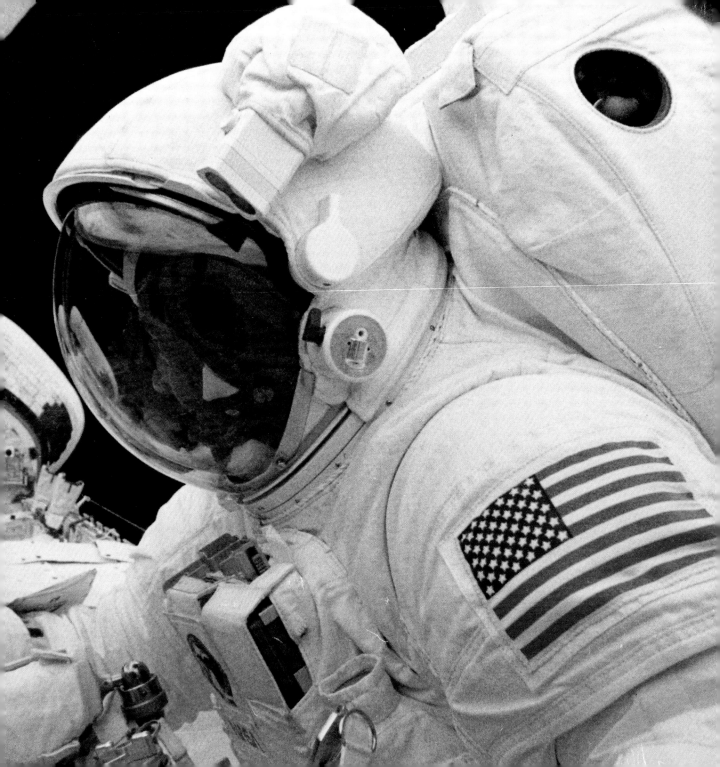

What Astronauts Wear

Astronauts wear uniforms inside a spacecraft. They wear space suits outside a spacecraft. Space suits cover their bodies. Helmets cover their heads. Space suits and helmets keep astronauts warm in space.

Tools Astronauts Use

Astronauts use cameras to take pictures in space. They take pictures of Earth. They also take pictures of stars and the moon. Everything floats in space. Special belts called tethers keep objects from floating away.

Astronauts and School

Astronauts must finish college. College is a place to study after high school. Astronauts take special classes after college. They learn about space. They learn what it is like to float in space.

Where Astronauts Work

Sometimes astronauts work in space. Other times they work at a space center. They train for space travel. Other astronauts use computers. They help to control spacecraft from the ground.

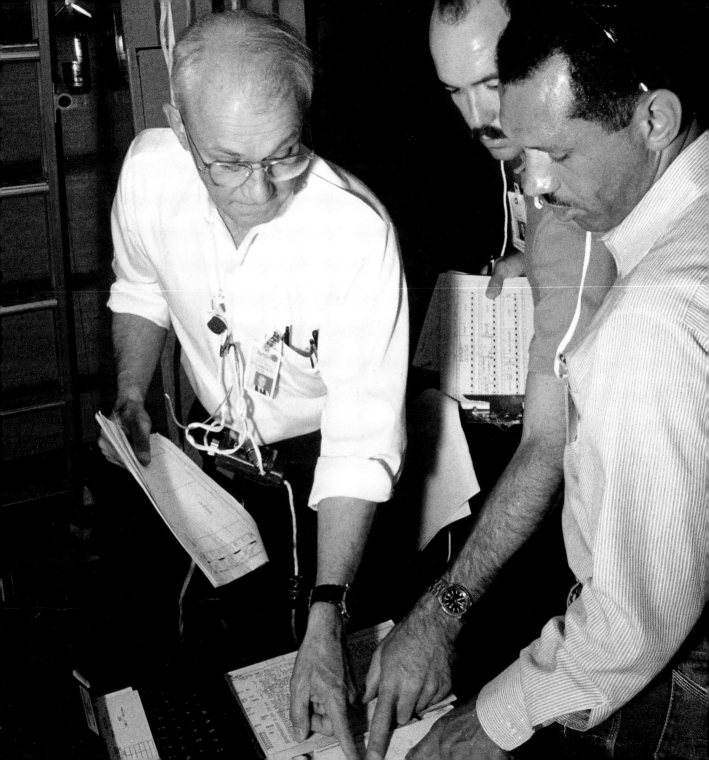

People Who Help Astronauts

Teachers help astronauts learn how to live in space. Workers in a space center also help astronauts. They help pilots fly and land spacecraft. They also help astronauts stay safe during space flights.

How Astronauts Help Others

Astronauts help people learn about space. They also help people learn about Earth. They take pictures of Earth from space. The pictures help people understand Earth.

Hands On: Drink without Gravity

There is no gravity in space. Gravity is the force that holds things to Earth. Many things are hard to do without gravity. Drinking water is hard to do in space. You can see what it is like to drink without gravity.

What You Need:

One glass of water
One chair

What You Do:

1. Put the glass of water on the floor. Put the chair next to it.
2. Lie across the chair on your back. Put your head near the floor. Your head must be lower than your stomach.
3. Try to drink the water.

It is hard to drink the water. Gravity pulls the water toward the floor. It is easier to drink standing up. Then gravity pulls the water down your throat.

Words to Know

experiment (ek-SPER-uh-ment)—a test to learn something new

gravity (GRAV-uh-tee)—the force that holds things to Earth

scientist (SYE-un-tist)—a person who does experiments

space suit (SPAYSS SOOT)—a suit that keeps an astronaut warm in space

Read More

Bredeson, Carmen. *Neil Armstrong : A Space Biography.* Springfield, N.J.: Enslow, 1998.

Mullane, R. Mike. *Liftoff!: An Astronaut's Dream.* Parsippany, N.J.: Silver Burdett Press, 1995.

Internet Sites

Ask an Astronaut
http://www.nss.org/askastro
The Astronaut Connection
http://www.nauts.com
Astronaut Training
http://www.geocities.com/CapeCanaveral/6098/training.htm

Index